Hi Beautiful Soul
Post pictures of your favourite images, pages,
affirmations and experiences related to this
book on social media using :

#BookOfLightOracle

So I can see them and share them on my page.

Thank you lovely xx

BOOK OF LIGHT

AN ORACLE BOOK OF UNIVERSAL GUIDANCE & AFFIRMATIONS

BY BLISS SUMMERS

BOOK OF LIGHT

Copyright © 2022 Bliss Summers

Published by Bliss Summers

Artwork and text by bliss summers

ISBN: 9798814532916

INTRODUCTION

Welcome beautiful souls, let this book of light inspire you to look deep within and connect to your true self and inner knowing allowing your intuition to flourish and bloom. Spirituality comes in all shapes and sizes, as does guidance from the angelic realm, the universe and your loved ones in spirit. Use this book to allow your senses to awaken and view your life and the glorious world around you from a greater spiritual perspective, one of fulfilment, joy and gratitude. Become more aware of your soul truth , true spiritual self and creative being. Your potential is limitless, you have a spiritual team comprising of the universe, the divine light, your spirit guides and your loved ones in spirit, supporting, guiding and loving you. Their love and guidance is abundant and transcends throughout the universe.

Energy is what gives every living soul life, this energy is light, a light that we all have individual to us, some brighter than others , a light that can be found in the stars , the moon, the sea and even a little bee.   This light connects us to our inner selves and even in the darkness light can be found. However dark a place maybe, there will always be light.

To harness your lights true potential you need to trust yourself, have faith and be open hearted. You need to open your mind, to the endless possibilities of the universe you are privileged to be in. You are worthy of greatness, love and abundance, now is the time to start seeing and believing in the light, which is you.

This little book of light, is here to remind you to take a step back, take a deep breath in and look deeper within yourself. You are so much more than a name, a number, a shape or a size, you are a gift from god, a star from the universe, a pure light that leads the way for others to follow. You are that shining light and now my dear it is your time to sparkle.

Lots of love and light Bliss x

HOW TO USE YOUR ORACLE BOOK

The Book Of Light Oracle Book, is an interactive oracle book filled with oracle messages, soul speak wisdom and daily affirmations.

This book has been lovingly created with the guidance of the universe, spirit and the angelic realm, to inspire you and provide you with daily messages, affirmations and guidance.

Your book has three sections, daily oracle messages, daily affirmations and soul speak wisdom. To receive your message and guidance, firstly select the oracle message section and close your eyes, let your finger tips run over the pages until you feel drawn to a page. Then select the page you feel drawn to and open your eyes. This page will have your oracle image and divine message on it. Once you have your oracle message it is now time for your daily affirmation, repeat the same process until you feel drawn to a page. Open your eyes and read your affirmation out loud or in your mind, projecting this beautiful intention into the universe for all to hear and align to you. The last section is soul speak, guidance from spirit and the universe, again close your eyes and select a page you feel drawn to. The message you receive might not be what you expect but what you need to hear at that time.

You can choose more than one oracle message, you will know when to stop. Connect to your inner-knowing as you do, you will get a feeling of how many pages to choose to answer your question or the person you are reading for. Trust your intuition, allow the divine light, spirit and universal energy to flow freely through your hands, and guide you.

☾

This is your oracle book, to receive the full benefits of this book you need to relax, clear your mind and open your heart to the love, light, and magic of the universe, spirit and angels. Utilise the magic from each page and the messages for you.

Be open throughout your reading to receiving the beautiful and uplifting energy that you will encounter, when using this special book. Each oracle page has a special message and meaning for you or the person you are reading for. As you bond and naturally connect with your book, you will find the right page presents itself at the right moment and for that person. When you have a clear bond with your book, you will be able to read intuitively from each page and trust your readings.

To prepare your book, it is good practice to cleanse your book before you use it, this is to cleanse any external or unwanted energy. This will also give you a fresh start and clean slate to enable you to bond with your book and each page. You can cleanse your book by using smudge spray, sage smudge stick, crystals, prayers and incense. These can be purchase at any spiritual shop or online.

The next step is to open your heart and mind to your book and form a connection. Take your book and place it firstly on your heart and then on the centre of your forehead where your third eye is. Then take your book and look at each page. Your eyes are the window to your soul and will help you truly connect to your book. Now you will have connected your heart, mind, and soul to your book. This will help connect your intuition to each page and the individual messages they have for you or the person you are reading for.

Once you have connected to your book, it is time to run through each page. Do this a few times or until your fingers feel at one with each page. Now you are ready to bless your book.

BLESS YOUR BOOK

Take your book and if you feel you want to, you can bless it. I like to bless mine before every reading. An example of a blessing I like to use is:

"Dear the divine light, angels and the universe, please hear me. Know as I open my heart, mind and soul to connect and work with your magic, white light, and love as I connect to this oracle book. Please guide me with love, light, and kindness. I open myself to this experience and your wisdom, spirit, and divine energy. Allow me to receive messages of love, light, and guidance. Help me connect to my destined soul path. Thank you for your divine light, love and energy."

You can use your own words, chants, or even sing if you like, there are no strict rules.

Blessing your book is a beautiful way of letting the divine light and universe know you are ready to connect and what your intention is. When using this book, as long as your intention is pure and from a place of love, light, and guidance your book will connect with you. Allow your words to flow free and easily, just speak from your heart and come from a place of love and light.

TAKE CARE OF YOUR BOOK

Who hasn't been hurt by the actions or words of another? Your book pages hold and absorb energy, which makes them very sensitive tools to work with. Because of this, it is important to store it in a safe or special place. You could keep it in a nice box or wrapped in a lovely cloth or pouch. Storing your book with crystals can also help to enhance its energy. Clear or rose quartz can add protection and love to your book. It can also be helpful to create a shield around your books pages, you can visualise your book in a bubble surrounded by purple and white light.

ASK YOUR QUESTION

There is always a reason you or someone else would like a reading and that is usually because they have a question, they would like help with. If that person is you, then take your book and ask your question over your book, either out loud or in your mind. If one or more pages jump out or catches your attention then these pages will form part of your reading. The same goes if you are reading for someone, however get them to ask the question over the book or in their mind.

When you are flicking through your pages and have asked your question, connect with the divine, spirit and the universe. Ask them to guide you and when to stop you when you arrive at the right page. They will show you by connecting to your senses, you might hear them speak, feel them, sense them or your inner knowing and just know when to stop. Trust your intuition.

Your book should become a part of you, like a favourite jumper or pair of fluffy socks, you want to wear over and over again. A friend that you trust and call on for advice, comfort, and truth.

The most important factor when reading from this book is that you have a natural and loving connection with it. This connection will grow and evolve over time. Your inner - knowing will resonate with each page naturally, and automatically understand and know what each message and page represents, when reading for yourself or someone else. Now you are ready to perform a reading with your book.

☾

GROUND AND PROTECT YOURSELF

When you connect to the powerful energy of The Book of Light Oracle, spirit, and your angels. It is especially important to ground and protect yourself. Prior to reading for yourself or others, it is advised you protect and ground yourself. This allows you to be more open and receptive to the energy you are receiving, which in turn will flow freely and enhance your intuition.

I like to use the following grounding practices: hold the book in your palm. Close your eyes and imagine you are in a beautiful and peaceful Forest. There is fresh bright sunlight forking through the leafy trees above you. Now focus on your feet and your toes, imagine that they are firmly on the ground. The ground feels soft and warm now the roots of the trees are around you, they are firmly around your toes and feet holding you steadily. Nothing can move you unless you say so. The trees are at one with you protecting and grounding you. You feel secure, relaxed, and sensitive to the elements around you. Now focus on your breathing, take in a deep breath and exhale all of your worries and stresses of the day. Now focus on imagining you are breathing in pure breaths of love and white light, repeat this until you feel your mind clear. Now whisper over the book or in your mind the following :

"Dear divine light, my angels, and loved ones in spirit. I ask for your love light, and protection as I open myself up to the magic and energy of this book. Thank you for your protection and white light."

You should feel a wash of love, light, and protection fall over you and you are now ready to start your reading.

DAILY READING

Your daily guidance one page oracle reading. This oracle reading is designed to set you up for the day and give you guidance on a question you have or a situation you are facing. I like to perform this reading first thing in the morning. Take your book and flick through your oracle pages, ask your questions or what you would like guidance on over your book or in your mind. When you feel ready choose a page that you are drawn to. Be open-minded to the guidance and message you receive. You are asking for advice and guidance, this can sometimes come as a surprise or not how you had viewed the situation. This is why we ask for support and guidance from a different unbiased perspective, from the divine and your loved ones in spirit. If you feel you need more depth to your reading, you can keep choosing pages you feel drawn to until you feel you have the answers and guidance you need. Remember to keep your question and situation at the forefront of your mind, as you continue to choose pages. You can also use this as a "now" instant reading if you need guidance there and then.

THREE CARD OVERVIEW

This reading is a three-page oracle reading and represents your Past, Present, and Future. These pages will focus on the energies in each of these areas. Flick through your pages and direct your energy and that of the divine with the intention of connecting to yourself or the person you are reading for Past, Present, and Future. When you feel connected select three pages you are drawn to.

Then working from left to right, hold your hand over each page and feel their energy, trust your intuition and begin your reading, in the order you prefer, to reveal their guidance and messages. Be mindful of future readings. The future is not final or set in stone, it changes and evolves as we do and its outcome changes based on our own outcomes and decisions made.

☾

DIVINE LIGHT INTUITIVE READING

This reading is based on using the divine light to guide you, this can be guidance for a situation, question, or general reading of what the next 6 months look like for you. This is a 7-page reading , each page has its own meaning. Flick through your oracle messages, set your intention to the forefront of your mind, and select seven pages that you are drawn to.

1) Your first page represents the situation and energy surrounding you at present.

2) Second page, what is happening or an indication of what could happen.

3) The third page, underlying energy behind your question or your desired outcome.

4) Fourth page, your next steps, direction, clarity and inspiration.

5) Fifth page, barriers that might hinder your desires or desired outcome of a situation.

6) Sixth page, represents your soul journey, path, and growth.

7) Seventh page, the possible result of your situation or desire. This outcome can vary depending on actions taken as your future is never set in stone.

ORACLE

GUIDANCE

STAR CHILD

The stars call you to love yourself, like the beautiful star you are. Self love will only make you shine brighter.

☾
STAR CHILD

The stars call you to love yourself, like the beautiful star you are. Self love will only make you shine brighter.

See the light in yourself and others. Don't let past hurt decide your future. Try star bathing, allow the magic to enter your mind and make a wish. You will be amazed at what can happen when you truly believe and give life to your dreams.

Have you ever seen a shooting star and had that magical moment when you make a wish? You feel the excitement, hope and anticipation of your wish coming true. This oracle is letting you know that you don't have to wait for a shooting star. You can have everything you wish for.

If you go through life with low expectations and expecting the worst the worst may happen. When you open yourself up to the endless possibilities and positive outcomes, you attract positive energy and abundance. Truly believe your wishes and dreams will come true. Ask your loved ones in spirit, your angels and spirit guides for help, support and guidance. Have faith in your ability to make your dreams a reality. The divine is working in the back ground but needs your faith to give life to your dreams and wishes. Your wishes are worth waiting for, truly believe you deserve everything you ask for and you will receive.

MOTHER EARTH

Each and every step we take is a connection and conversation with mother earth. Take some time to be with her.

MOTHER EARTH

Each and every step we take is a connection and conversation with mother earth. Take some time to be with her.

Patience is a virtue. Divine timing is at work trust that all is well and your dreams are manifesting.

Use this time to relax and reflect on what you really want. Now is not the time to rush into anything, such as a project, relationship or business venture. You may be feeling frustrated that nothing is happening and want to get the ball rolling, but hold off just for now. Mother earth takes her time creating new life, each season perfected, ever changing and evolving.

Everything happens for a reason and the divine is working their magic. The results will come to light very soon. You have set clear intentions and asked the universe for fulfilment of your dreams. Now let manifesting take place and allow all to materialise.

Everything happens at the right time in the right place. Conserve your efforts and energy just a little while longer and you will be rewarded. Take time out to ground yourself and connect back to yourself and mother earth.

☾

MESSAGE

Talk to your loved ones and angels above. You will receive a message when you least expect it but need it the most.

MESSAGE

Talk to your loved ones and angels above. You will receive a message when you least expect it but need it the most.

You will receive a message when you least expect it but need it the most. Look out for the signs.

Your loved ones in spirit and your guardian angels have been trying to contact you and send you messages of love, light, support and guidance.
You may have seen white feathers, smelt different smells or a loved one's fragrance. You might have seen something in the corner of your eye, heard significant music or felt a loved one's presence around you.

Feel rest assured they are safe and well. They are watching over you and will continue to send you signs and messages. Be open minded to the messages your receive and to the messenger themselves. Talk to them and ask them for help with your troubles and worries. They are always with and around you and love you very much.

ROMANCE

We receive what we project. Stay optimistic, keep your heart open. Positive thinking will bring love and romance into your life.

☾

ROMANCE

We receive what we project. Stay optimistic, keep your heart open. Positive thinking will bring love and romance into your life.

Romance is returning into your life and relationships. You are worthy of love and how you want to be loved. Prepare for your life partner. This oracle is asking you to open yourself up to receiving love and to the universe to attract love and loving relationships.

Learn to love yourself, when we love every part of ourselves including our imperfections we shine from within and attract love, kindness and joy. By loving every part of you, you do not project negative thoughts about yourself on to other people. When you make a connection with another person, they will reflect what you project and love every part of you also.

Know your worth, stop putting yourself down, you are loveable and beautiful inside and out, let your love shine from within. You are a very kind, caring and loving person, who offers pure unconditional love. Don't let love constrain or restrict you, a loving relationship should be mutual, free and flowing, allowing you both to grow and evolve in line with your soul journey. A relationship is a partnership working in harmony with each other.

If you are in a relationship currently, this oracle is asking you to renew your passion and deepen your connection. Find those extra minutes to talk, go on that date, embrace that hug or hold their hand. Take time to understand why you connected in the first place and how your love blossomed, plant new seeds of love for each other and watch them grow and bloom over again.

☾

SOUL PATH

What makes your soul sing? Turn off the noise of the
world, talk and listen to your soul, you already have
the answer.

SOUL PATH

Ever changing, ever evolving, ever you. Prepare for a change.

Your soul journey is evolving and your life's purpose changing. Embrace a welcome and blessed career change.

Do you feel like you are standing still, unsure if you are in the right place or bored doing the same thing over and over again?

Well get ready because life is about to become exciting! This oracle is asking you to look at all the things you want to do in your career and life and set them into motion.

The divine has been hard at work behind the scenes, and you are finally ready to take the leap of faith you have been waiting for. Don't worry about trying something new, really stretch yourself. Look at what you need to do to get you to where you want to be. Sign up for that class and learn something new, try a new activity, raise your confidence levels. You will find learning new skills, will help you in all areas of your life, not just your career.

FEED YOUR SOUL

You are what you eat, feed and nourish your soul
with goodness.

☽

FEED YOUR SOUL

You are what you eat, feed and nourish your soul with goodness.

You have a pure heart and with this comes powerful healing gifts. Stop doubting your abilities, embrace and develop your gifts. follow your soul journey.

Feed your soul, with love, laughter and positive energy. It is so easy to feed ourselves with self doubt , criticism and envy.

Everyone has a natural ability to heal others and themselves. Be open to receiving healing and embracing your healing gifts. Healing comes in many forms from psychical energy healing to simply listening to someone in need, without judgment just love and a shared understanding.

Holding people in your thoughts and sharing healing thoughts and feelings out to the universe, is also a powerful healing tool for people to receive.

This oracle is asking you to develop your skills further and acknowledge the love you share when you heal others.

This oracle is also asking you to listen to your body, understand what it is telling you. Get more rest, sleep or nourishment. To heal others, we must first heal ourselves and ensure our bodies and minds are in optimum health. Feed your soul the goodness of the world around you and you will notice the difference soul food can make to your life.

PROGRESSION

Baby steps, your steps, my steps, our steps. A
journey shared is a milestone gained.

PROGRESSION

Baby steps, your steps, my steps, our steps. A journey shared is a milestone gained.

All will become clear when the time is right. It is never too late to learn something new.

Knowledge is not only power, but the freedom to make an informed choice, a choice that will allow you to take those precious steps forward.

Sometimes we are left with a decision to make, and we find ourselves struggling to make the right decision. Don't let other people influence your decision. Make the decision what is best for you right now.

This decision could be regarding family, career, relationships, finances, or life direction. Listen to your intuition and ask spirit and your guides for help.

Now is the time to take that next step and discover more. Expand your mind and knowledge, join a group, book a course, talk to someone, get some books, and learn. Then only when you feel ready, make your informed choice and take your first step forward.

🌙

RELEASE

Honour your emotions and embrace the freedom.

RELEASE

Honour your emotions and embrace the freedom

Anger is a powerful force. Turn this force into a positive one. Honour all of your emotions, as you safely express your anger and embrace the feeling of release.

Anger is a powerful force, if bottled up can erupt at unexpected moments and be a destructive force leaving devastation and hurt in its wake. Harness your anger and use it positively.

You may be feeling angry at life, yourself, family or at a situation. Anger is one of four key emotions such as love, hope and happiness and just as important. Anger is a strong emotion and should not be bottle up, but expressed safely.

Anger can be the driving force that lifts you up to take action and push forward with your plan or set boundaries in place to stop people disempowering or walking all over you.
 Acknowledge and use your anger to release and unleash any fears you have and unearth any hurt you have been carrying around with you. As long as you release your anger in a safe way and not misdirected at anyone else, feel empowered and release all of your anger. Dance, run, climb, yodel, shout in the middle of a field, yell and scream out all of your anger.

 Give your heart permission to fully feel, grieve and then release, releasing your anger in this cathartic way will leave you feeling refreshed, empowered and lift a weight off your shoulders, because you are no longer holding on to rage, but positive renewed energy, pushing you forward.

FULL MOON

Embrace the energy of the moon, every situation
has a cycle.

☾

FULL MOON

Embrace the energy of the moon, every situation has a cycle

The Moon energy is working in your favour, you deserve this chance do not let it pass you by.

Take delight in the new opportunities that present themselves. You deserve this chance. Don't let it pass you by. This oracle is asking you to be prepared, unexpected opportunities will present themselves.

The divine has been working hard with the universe to answer your prayers and provide you with solutions to your problems. Sometimes opportunities present themselves and we let them pass us by.

You might feel that you are afraid of the change that comes with these new possibilities, you might be worried about the financial implication, home work life balance or you might not feel you have the confidence to make the move at your time in your life.

This oracle is here to remind you that you have the support, love, and guidance for your loved ones in spirit, angels, and spirit guides.

Rest assured the divine light would never present you with an opportunity you could not handle. Remember your soul journey is to love, learn and live. When this opportunity presents itself to you, take a moment and ask your heart, intuition and guides for guidance's and trust your inner knowing that you deserve this chance, don't let fear stop you.

WELCOME HOME

Love, joy and laughter are returning to your life.

☾

WELCOME HOME

Love, joy and laughter are returning to your life

Now is the time to enjoy the moment. Good times await you, bringing joy and laughter back into your life.

Love, joy, and laughter have been missing recently, this oracle is asking you to take your serious hat off and replace it with joy and optimism.

You have been through some stressful situations and each one taken a toll on you. You have been feeling stressed, overwhelmed or unhappy recently.

The divine is sending you lots of love, joy and laughter your way. Now is the time to step away from stress, anxiety and find the fun and humour in life and each new situation that comes your way.

Every time you find laughter in a difficult situation you are choosing a better way forward, a choice that helps heal you along the way. This oracle is asking you to socialise more, arrange fun activities, meet up with friends, phone your family for a chat, book a holiday or go for a walk with a friend.

When we laugh, we release stress, tension and anger, which enables us to relax and connect to our inner selves. Laughter is the best medicine and beautiful soul therapy.

EMBRACE THE BLOOM

Dare to dream a beautiful dream and you shall receive.

☾

EMBRACE THE BLOOM

Dare to dream a beautiful dream and you shall receive

A happy surprise is on its way to you. Your prayers have been answered and your angels and guides are watching over you.
Your dreams are materialising. This oracle wants you to fill your heart and soul with joy and excitement, a beautiful and well needed surprise is on its way to you.

The beauty of a surprise is the actual surprise, do not try and guess or unearth your surprise. Know that it comes with love and from the highest light. Your prayers have been heard and your wish granted.

Remember the divine light will provide you with what you need when you least expect it but need it the most. Gifts come in many shapes and forms, from a simple but beautiful act of kindness, a new opportunity, increase in income, reduction in outgoings, an answered prayer, to long awaited good news.

If we always expect the best and share our dreams, hopes and prayers out to the universe they will be heard, sharing is caring, and self-love is crucial.

You are your soul's vessel and need to be cherished. Give thanks and gratitude to every gift you receive from a beautiful morning sunrise to the full moon in the sky. The more thankful we are, the more gifts we will receive.

SKIN DEEP

See the light in yourself and others.

SKIN DEEP

See the light in yourself and others. Don't let past hurt decide your future.

Soften your heart and forgive those who have built your walls up. Forgiveness is the best gift you can give and will set you free. The world is a better place with love, light and forgiveness.

This world has evolved into one where we are judged on perceived perfection. It is so easy to look at the people around you and want to compare their success, appearance and life style with yours. This is your life, your soul journey, don't judge a book by its cover.

Life is a beautiful experience, individual and unique to each and every one of us. Try not to compare yourself to others they have their own soul path to follow.

Your soul journey is not a race, competition or judgment. Follow your own destiny your way and view yourself how the divine light does, perfect in every way, beautiful inside and out, stronger that you know and very much loved. Relinquish any negative feelings you have about yourself; release any guilt or feelings of doubt or resentment you hold over yourself.

Forgive yourself for all of your mistakes or missed opportunities, this will set you free and remember there is always a reason you are in the right place at the right moment. This is your journey, and you are here to learn, love and live your life. Open your heart to receiving compassion and love, let it flow through you and spread to everyone worldwide. True miracles are created when we share love, kindness and compassion.

DIVINE FEMININE ENERGY

Now is your time to bloom.

☾

DIVINE FEMININE ENERGY

Now is your time to bloom

Allow positive divine feminine energy to enter your life, embrace your curves, perfect imperfect edges and celebrate you. Love every part of you and allow all negative self-thoughts to wash away. You do not need to be thinner, taller, bigger lips or a smaller nose in order to embody your true divine feminine energy. She comes from within, when you fully embrace her she shines through you, in your eyes and smile.

You have the power inside you to change your world and make miracles happen. You are a radiator radiating love, light and abundance, people are drawn to you and new opportunities are aligning with your true self.

You are beautiful inside and out, so much stronger than you know and very much loved. Do not listen to others who tell you differently or let them disempower you, they are like drains and you want to be sounded by radiators, radiating the same self-love as you.

We Live in a world where perfection is deemed to define us and our beauty defined by the media and flavour of the month, never really being able to connect to our true selves. Always trying to evolve into someone that is unnatural and a million miles away from our true self.
Your style is unique, your features chosen just for you and your beautiful personality created to inspire others. Never let anyone dull your sparkle, every mark on our body and hearts is a reminder of where we have come from. These marks do not define us, they only add to our experience library and inner fullness.

Step forward into the light, head held high like a warrior fearless to the world, let your self-love shield you from the negativity of the world and let the world see your true colours. Wear these colours with pride and in doing so, you will inspire others to reconnect to their divine feminine energy and bloom together with you.

DIAMONDS ARE...

Rocks with potential, harness your potential and do what diamonds do best, shine.

DIAMONDS ARE...

Rocks with potential, harness your potential and do what diamonds to best , shine.

Look at your situation do you feel overwhelmed and in over your head? Do you feel you want to break free?

You are a diamond in the rough waiting to break free, it is your time to shine, you have been hiding your talent, your true self for too long. You are not a rock to be stood on or passed by, you are a diamond, do what diamonds do best, sparkle and shine!

It may have been easier for you to hide away in the background to fit in, you may have taken on everyone else's opinions, views and beliefs other than your own. Well now is your time to rise up, crack open and reveal yourself to the world, let everyone see your inner beauty and powerful glow.

When we connect to our own truth we naturally shine from within, people and abundance will be drawn to you.

This oracle is letting you know that you are in control, you have the power to change your current situation a world of opportunities awaits you, they are ready for you and YOU are ready for them.

FAMILY

Your soul family awaits you, different, beautiful, yours.

☾

FAMILY

Your soul family awaits you, different, beautiful, yours

Your soul family awaits you. Surround yourself with positive and grounded people. Families are built on trust. Trust the ones you love. Socialise more and your family will grow.

Family, no one family are the same, a family doesn't have to be the perfect nuclear family of two adults and two children.

Your family can be a social family of friends, relatives and animals. Families are made up of a community with one common denominator that is love. They love each other, they support and guide each other.

You have an earth family and as we grow older this turns into a soul family. Your loved ones are still here to support love and guide you. Your loved ones in spirit want you to know that they love you, they are safe and well and will always be with you.

This oracle also wants to know that your family loves you very much. Families argue and have difference of opinions, that does not mean they do not love you, they want the best for you.

COURAGEOUS HEART

Do not let fear control who you are.

COURAGEOUS HEART

Do not let fear control who you are

You are courageous, you have the power to set strong boundaries and stand up for your beliefs. Do not let fear control who you are.

Sometimes we find ourselves in situations where there is no other choice but to be courageous. This oracle is asking you to approach your situation with love, courage and self-belief.

You can do this and no matter the outcome, you have the love and support of your loved ones in spirit, angels and spirit guides. Don't let fear hold you back or allow it to lower your vibration.

Remember who you are, what you came here to do and where you are supposed to be. This is your world, your life, it is time to step in to the light and shine.

Don't let other people's beliefs or negativity paint a future with limited potential and outcomes. Approach the world knowing that it is full of love, light, kindness and endless opportunities for you to grow and evolve.

When you have true self believe, courage comes naturally and will guide you safely to where you are supposed to be.

ENERGY BLOCK

Follow your intuition and manifest your dreams.

ENERGY BLOCK

Follow your intuition and manifest your dreams

Follow your intuition and manifest your dreams into reality. Manage your finances with love, a gift is on its way.

Happy news and financial blessings are on their way to you. This oracle asks you to open yourself up to receiving abundance.

You may have had financial blocks in the past or have been asking for financial advice from the divine, your loved ones and your guardian angels.

Now is the time to give gratitude and thanks for the financial abundance you have been manifesting and are about to receive. Organise and manage your finances and accounts with love, regardless of the amount you currently have.

Being grateful and thankful will send positive vibrations out to the universe, and increase your levels of abundance and prosperity in return. Opportunities for your income to increase and all your material needs met in abundance, are on there way to you, allow prosperity to flow into your life.

MAKING PEACE

The gift of forgiveness. Let go, be free ,
find your peace.

☾

MAKING PEACE

The gift of forgiveness. Let go, be free , find your peace

Forgiveness is the best gift you can give or receive. Now is the time for letting go of anger or guilt.

Who hasn't been hurt by the actions or words of another? This oracle is asking you to forgive people around you and also yourself.

Forgiveness is not about forgetting or excusing the harm done to you or letting people walk all over you.

Forgiveness is about releasing the negative emotion, resentment and vengeance caused by the hurt. These emotions are powerful and extremely draining. By forgiving yourself and others, you are releasing these emotions and opening yourself up to peace, hope, gratitude and joy.

In today's world we are so quick to criticise ourselves, our appearance, parenting skills, decisions, pasts, the list goes on. Forgive yourself, stop thinking about the should a, could a, would a.

 You did the best you could, at that moment, with what you had. Choose forgiveness and let go of all the excess.

ALTAR

Where you start is not always where you end. Embrace change.

☾

ALTAR

Where you start is not always where you end. Embrace change

What do you want? What are your priorities? Focus on the outcome you desire, and the motivation you require will come.

This oracle asks you to stop spinning all those plates and spreading yourself too thinly.

When people ask you what do you want? Do you struggle to give them a direct and simple response back? Do you give an answer then add but I don't have time for that or it will never happen?

Now is the time for you to act and focus on your priorities and what you truly desire and want in your life.

Stop putting boundaries in the way and don't let other people decide what your priorities are or should be. This is your life, your soul journey and your opportunity to prioritise yourself and your happiness.

Rise up and take the hand of the divine, let it lift you up and place you on the pedestal you deserve. Allow yourself to manifest the life, job, relationship, career, education you want, feel the motivation and positive energy flow freely through you. The next step you take will be the one you choose to take.

EMBRACE THE CLEANSE

Prepare for physical and emotional healing.

☾

EMBRACE THE CLEANSE

Prepare for physical and emotional healing

Take a step back to honour your feelings and emotions. You are sensitive to the energies and emotions around you.

Do not let them drain you. Emotions can be both beautiful and powerful. This oracle asks you to approach this situation differently.

Take a step back, the emotions you feel right now need time to adjust. When we love someone, we feel protective over them and when they hurt, we hurt. This emotion can cloud our judgment in that moment.

This oracle also resonates with the saying we hurt the people we are closest to, when we love someone, this could be parents, siblings, children, friends we feel relaxed and safe with them. This can lead us to sometimes misdirect our frustration and raw emotion onto them.

Know that they love you and understand. Everything in this beautiful world is made up of energy including emotion. If you are sensitive to other people's emotions and have a gift such as an empath, take time to protect yourself and your emotions, from absorbing other people's emotional energy. This can be both draining, confusing and frustrating.

Know that you are in control, set boundaries and don't let other people's emotional energy make decisions for you.

FORGOTTEN KINGDOM

Unveil the passion you lost and make love to the
how, when and where.

FORGOTTEN KINGDOM

Unveil the passion you lost and make love to the how, when and where.

Unveil the passion you lost and make love to the how, when and where. Find and ignite your passion. Doing what excites you, will invite new energy into your relationship, career, and life.

A life without passion is not a life at all. This oracle is telling you to ignite and find your passion. Do what excites you, ignore other people's views and get fired up about your life.

Life is a beautiful and exciting adventure, why settle for less when you can have more, more fun, more adventure, more laughter. This oracle is filling your heart and life with energy, enthusiasm and pure passion to kick start your dreams. It is your time start living and pursue your passions in both your career and personal life.

Do you want to changes jobs? Work with animals, move location, travel the world, set up a business, try a new sport, get involved with a charity, change who you are and make a difference in the world?

Now is the time shake off the dust, worry and lacklustre routine and be like the sun, shine brightly and leave the shadows behind you. Now is your time to be truly fabulous darling, live your life by your own rules.

This oracle is also telling you to take care of yourself, increase your energy levels, drink more water, eat more healthily, get more rest. When your body feels good so do you. This will allow you to give 100% to your life, passions and invite new and beautiful relationships into your life.

GARDEN OF ROSES

Don't let your thorns stop you from blooming.

☾

GARDEN OF ROSES

Don't let your thorns stop you from blooming

Dare to step into the unknown. Take a leap of faith and start your own adventure. Manifest your dreams of traveling, moving house, starting a new business, or starting a family.

Do something that makes your heart sing and soul dance. This oracle is asking you to step out of your routine, turn left instead of right.

Follow your heart and intuition instead of your head. Stop conforming to everyone else's social norms and values.

This is your life, your moment your opportunity to embark on a new venture, travel the world, start a movement, support a charity, start a family or new career.

This oracle also means, try something new however little that may be, from taking the scenic route on a journey to trying a new recipe or a different walk.

Trying something new each day, keeps your soul alive and your heart young. Breathe in and embrace change however small it may be. This will allow you and your soul to evolve, grow and shine.

MOTHER

Blind Love is unconditional, heals fear, gives faith and fulfilment.

MOTHER

Blind Love is unconditional, heals fear, gives faith and fulfilment

All you need is love, love heals fear, gives faith and fulfilment. Give Love to yourself and be open to receiving love from others around you.

From being born to the day that we pass over to spirit, all we want is to feel is unconditional love. Love comes in many forms from your parents, spouse, children and animals.

It is important to open your heart to receiving love and believing that you are worthy of love. Sometimes when we are afraid of rejection or have a fear of not being loved, this in turn can make us feel angry or closed off.

Anger comes from fear, try not to respond with anger but with love instead, show them they are safe.

Also remember that people have different love languages. These love languages consist of words, gifts, touch, acts and giving of time.

Your love language might be to give and receive gifts. Another person's love language, might be to show affection or give up their time to help you with tasks you might have. These different love languages don't mean that a person loves you any less, they just express their love in a different way.

Always remember you are beautiful inside and out, stronger than you know and very much loved. Embrace the mothers love of the divine and all she has to offer.

PORTAL

This is your future which door will you choose.

☾

PORTAL

This is your future which door will you choose.

This is your future. Take action to enable your ideas and dreams to come to fruition. You have spirit and angels guiding and supporting you.

This oracle is asking you to give life to your ideas, dreams and follow your soul path. You might want to set up a new business venture, start a new social group, set up a charity, join a new activity, solve a work issue or family situation.

The time is right for you to act now, have faith you will succeed and you will. Set your intention for success, positive energy and a beautiful outcome for all involved. Don't let other people's views or material issues stop you from setting your dreams and ideas in motion.

The divine is working behind the scenes, supporting and guiding you through this transition. This is the beginning of something truly beautiful, take a deep breath and step forward in to the light. Let the light wash over you and fill your heart and soul with excitement, joy and anticipation of what is to come.

Everything starts off as a little thought an idea or dream, each a little seed that has been planted waiting to grow and bloom. Idea's change the world, they save lives and allow economies to evolve and the world to progress. What will your idea do?

☽

SISTERHOOD

Bonds bound can never be broken.

☾

SISTERHOOD

Bonds bound can never be broken

Your soul sisters are calling you; they are urging you to pick up the phone and call them. Being around like-minded friends is what you need to elevate you to the next level.

You may have frustrations you need to vent or ideas you need to share or just need a cup of tea and a hug. True friendships last a life time, these friendships endure highs and lows but always stay strong.

 A soul sister is someone who knows you inside out, someone you can rely on and tell your deepest secrets and desires and be truthful and honest, a true equal. Sometimes a soul sister can come into your life unexpectedly, by chance even. This is when you know she was sent to you when you least expected her but needed her the most.

As we align with our soul path and destiny, we send vibrations out to the universe and in return we attract new and beautiful energies into our life, these energies come to us in the form of soul sisters.

Remember your soul sister can enter your life at any stage. If you have lost contact with one of your soul sisters this oracle is a gentle reminder to reach out and strengthen your bond. Now is the time to allow new soul sisters to enter your life. Open your heart to new friendships, new possibilities, it is ok to be vulnerable, your soul sister will never let you fall, her arms are open, and bonds bound can never be broken.

SOUL SPEAK

Listen to your soul and rhythm of your heart,
absorb kindness.

SOUL SPEAK

Listen to your soul and rhythm of your heart, absorb kindness

Be gentle with yourself and surround yourself with kind people. Focus on situations and environments with positive energy.

This oracle is connecting to a gentle soul, sometimes the busy world can feel overwhelming at times making you feel like a spare part or unable to connect with your peers.

You may feel like you want to retreat or head to a quiet place surrounded by nature, animals and wildlife. You have a sensitive caring nature and beautiful and natural connections with animals. Emotions come easily to you and you can sometimes wear your heart on your sleeve.

You are sensitive to the different energies and emotions around you, these in turn indicate that you have strong psychic and intuitive abilities such as an empath.

Try to embrace your gifts and not worry about what others think. Your gentle soul and calming nature shines through and you may feel uncomfortable addressing conflict, intimidating situations or standing up for yourself. Now is the time to act with courage strength and understanding, shower them with your gentle kindness.

Lead by example and show your peers, family, friends and the world that love and kindness can conquer all. This is not a sign of weakness but a sign of strength and doing things differently.

WINDOW

Who is the mirror to your soul prepare for
your spiritual awakening.

WINDOW

Who is the mirror to your soul prepare for your spiritual awakening

Find your twin flame, your mirror soul. You have an intense connection with them that is both healing and challenging.

This oracle is asking you to relax and enter the doors of your spiritual awakening. Connect to your heart and feel the energy, love and truth of your twin flame. A twin flame is your mirror soul, they reflect back to you, your weaknesses but also your greatest strengths.

They help you with your pain, challenge you and enable you to heal. When you find your twin flame, you immediately feel whole again, content and transition into a journey of personal growth and transformation.

Finding your twin flame is a gift from the divine, grasp it with both hands. Allow them to let you release all of the baggage you have been carrying from the past, it no longer serves you and is weighing you down.

Now is the time to find your higher self and connect to your true purpose.

YOUR GIFT

Now is the time to embrace your gifts.

YOUR GIFT

Now is the time to embrace your gifts

You have a gift, now is the time to embrace your gifts. Ask for support and guidance to help develop your natural-born talent.

You have been born with a beautiful gift this could be the gift of creativity, counselling, singing, connecting with spirit or inspiring others.

You may have pursued your gifts before but felt pressure from other people who did not show you support or understanding. You might not know what your gift is, this is your opportunity to try new and exciting things. You will never know what beautiful and amazing gifts you have, if you never explore or try new things.

This oracle is calling you to express yourself and use your gifts, go forth without fear and develop your gifts, use them and show them off to their full potential, you were given these gifts for a purpose. They are special and unique to you.

🌙

YOUR TIME IS NOW

Speak your mind and own your truth. Rise and you shall not fall.

YOUR TIME IS NOW

Speak your mind and own your truth. Rise and you shall not fall

It's your time to show the world who you really are and what you are made of. Don't be afraid to share your message. You are a diamond and now is your time to shine.

Now is the time for you to truly shine. You are beautiful inside and out, talented and truly unique. Don't be afraid to show who you really are, speak your mind and own your truth, now is your time to embrace your own success.

You are individual and don't need to be like everyone else. You have been waiting for this moment just like a butterfly, your soul is calling for you to spread your wings and share your message and fly. Your potential is limitless, don't be afraid to fly high and soar.

Don't let anyone hold you back or weigh you down, they don't have the courage to follow you. Show them the way by following your soul path.

Nurture yourself and prepare for your journey of a life time, let yourself expand, the world is ready for your greatness. You are a diamond, you cannot be broken, do what diamond's do best and shine brightly.

TIME

You are a Queen Bee and just like her, you will choose your own battles. Do not be led by others, make your own choices.

☾
TIME

You are a Queen Bee and just like her, you will choose your own battles. Do not be led by others, make your own choices.

Listen to your feelings and the divine light guiding you. Trust your natural-born intuition to help guide you and your heart.

Now is the time to trust your inner-knowing, these are the whispers of your heart and soul, your "gut feeling". It's about time you start believing in yourself and trusting your intuition.

Have you felt yourself saying I knew that would happen, I knew they were no good, I knew that wasn't right? Trusting your intuition is a powerful tool to help guide and support you in life and on your soul journey.

Your inner- knowing gives you insight to what could be and is a soul compass to guide you in the right direction. Sometimes we ignore our intuition and dismiss them as silly thoughts because we don't want to accept the truth.

Sometimes we are frightened of things we cannot control, your intuition is your key to freedom, the freedom of knowing what is going to happen based on the choices you make before you commit to them.

Try not to waste time rationalising your instincts or inner knowing because deep down you know it is right. Learn to trust yourself and have confidence that your intuition is guiding you to the right place at the right moment.

DAILY

AFFIRMATIONS

☾

AFFIRMATIONS HELP REMIND US WHO WE ARE,
WHAT WE ARE CAPABLE OF AND HELP PROJECT
AND TRANSMIT POSITIVE ENERGY OUT TO THE
UNIVERSE, HELPING US ATTRACT POSITIVE
ENERGY AND ABUNDANCE IN RETURN.

☾

MONEY FLOWS TO ME EASILY AND ABUNDANTLY.

- Bliss Summers

☾

I BREATHE IN POSITIVITY, ABUNDANCE
AND LOVE. I EXHALE FEAR, PAIN AND
WORRY.

- Bliss Summers

I AM WORTHY OF LOVE AND ABUNDANCE.

- Bliss Summers

I ACCEPT EVERY PART OF ME JUST THE
WAY I AM.

- Bliss Summers

☾

SOMETHING WONDERFUL IS ABOUT TO HAPPEN TO ME.

- Bliss Summers

☾

ABUNDANCE, LOVE AND LIGHT
GRAVITATE TO ME.

- Bliss Summers

I SHINE FROM WITHIN

- Bliss Summers

☾

I HAVE THE POWER TO CHANGE MY WORLD

- Bliss Summers

OPPORTUNITY ALIGNS WITH ME, EASILY AND EFFORTLESSLY

- Bliss Summers

I CALL AND PROTECT MY ENERGY, FOR
IT BELONGS TO ME.

- Bliss Summers

☾

I AM BLESSED, WHOLE AND VERY MUCH LOVED

- Bliss Summers

I HAVE THE POWER TO CHANGE MY LIFE.

- Bliss Summers

☾

I ATTRACT POSITIVE ENERGY

- Bliss Summers

I AM DIVINE. I AM BEAUTIFUL. I AM
BLESSED. I AM WHOLE AND I AM LOVED.

- Bliss Summers

I CHOOSE TO ALIGN WITH THE BEST
VERSION OF MYSELF AT EVERY
MOMENT.

- Bliss Summers

I AM ABUNDANT WITH LOVE, LIGHT AND POSITIVITY.

- Bliss Summers

☾

I AM BLESSED. I MANIFEST WITH EASE AND I ALIGN WITH PURE SUCCESS.

- Bliss Summers

ALL I WANT AND ALL I NEED, FLOWS
TO ME WITH EASE.

- Bliss Summers

☾

I CALL TO ME, THE ENERGY OF PROSPERITY.

- Bliss Summers

☾

I CALL TO ME, THE ENERGY OF ABUNDANCE.

- Bliss Summers

I AM WHOLE, I AM HEALTHY, MY SOUL
IS ENRICHED AND MY BODY IS LOVED.

- Bliss Summers

I DECIDE WHICH DOOR TO OPEN,
NOT EVERY DOOR DESERVES
MY ATTENTION.

- Bliss Summers

☾

I RAISE MY VIBRATION TO ATTRACT ALL THAT I NEED AND WANT.

- Bliss Summers

☾

I AM READY TO FIND LOVE AND BE LOVED.

- Bliss Summers

☾

THAT WHICH SERVES ME, FLOWS TO ME EASILY.

- Bliss Summers

THE UNIVERSE WILL PROVIDE ME
WITH ALL THAT I DESIRE.

- Bliss Summers

I INVITE ABUNDANCE INTO MY LIFE.

- Bliss Summers

🌙

I AM STRONG. POWERFUL. BEAUTIFUL
AND LOVED.

- Bliss Summers

☾

THE MORE POSITIVITY I RADIATE THE MORE I WILL RECEIVE

- Bliss Summers

I WAS BORN TO SUCCEED AND ATTRACT ALL THAT I NEED.

- Bliss Summers

MONEY, ABUNDANCE AND LOVE FLOW EASILY TO ME.

- Bliss Summers

I INVITE HEALTH, WEALTH, LOVE AND
LIGHT INTO MY LIFE.

- Bliss Summers

☽

MY SOUL GROWS AND VIBRATION RISES AND WITH THAT LOVE FLOWS TO ME.

- Bliss Summers

☾

I ATTRACT HEALTH, WEALTH AND ALIGN WITH THE POWER OF THE DIVINE.

- Bliss Summers

I CALL BACK LOST ENERGY. I HARNESS MY POWER AND LET GO OF NEGATIVE THOUGHTS.

- Bliss Summers

☾

I CALL TO ME, THE ENERGY OF LOVE AND ABUNDANCE.

- Bliss Summers

I ALIGN WITH THE ENERGY OF
PROSPERITY AND ABUNDANCE.

- Bliss Summers

☾

THAT WHICH SERVES ME, FLOWS EASILY TO ME.

- Bliss Summers

☽

MY SOUL IS CONNECTED TO THE PLENTIFUL ABUNDANCE OF THE UNIVERSE.

- Bliss Summers

SOUL

SPEAK

Even Trees Have Stretchmarks

It was a Saturday morning and I went for a forest walk with my little ones to collect leaves and reconnect to mother nature. I had been feeling a little down regarding my appearance and general confidence, having gained weight and the delights of getting older. As this thought popped into my head I saw spirit appear next to this very tree (spirit have a habit of doing this!)

It was my twin sister this time. She was laughing at me, she showed me this beautiful tree and said "don't be silly, even trees get stretch marks see. We can't be forever young and why would we want too? The difference is, this tree wears his stretch marks and perfect imperfections with pride. No one is perfect, not even this beautiful tree and that is the beauty of it. It is a map of your bodies journey. This tree from a tiny sapling to a tall towering tree watching over the forest. Yours, your precious children and individual journey, every year that passes is a year filled with life lessons and wisdom gained".

I let my fingers touch and gently run over the trees stretch marks, my eyes following the individual network of ridges and furrow. As my eyes reached the top I felt a warm wash of energy flow over me. She was right (as always).

 *Your Spirit Message*

Whenever you feel a little down or you start to question yourself. You are perfect just the way you are, wear your scars visible and invisible, your curves, lumps, bumps and insecurities with pride and turn them into parts of yourself that you love. These are your individual perfect imperfections no one but you have these, so lets just embrace them.

No one looks like your beautiful self, or has your radiant soul, you are more than beautiful, you are you, which is more than enough. Sending you so much love, light heavenly hugs and a shower of heavenly confidence.

Water And Spirit

Did you know that your body is made up of up to 75% water? Water also has memory and reacts to the emotions and environment it is in.

Water is a symbol of Purity, Clarity, and Receptiveness. Spirit love water. I always make sure I have a full glass by my bedside.

Water helps you connect to the earth. Just think how many people, animals, trees and the list goes on, that glass of water you are about to drink has gone through.

Since water is clear, it reflects whoever or whatever is looking into it, like a mirror does. Ever heard that saying mirror mirror on the wall, who is the fairest of them all?

Looking at water encourages you to reflect, by helping you listen to, and understand, your thoughts and emotions. Through that process you can become more aware of the state of your soul and soul journey.

I was on a walk and came across this river and I had the overwhelming urge to dip my hand into the water. It felt amazing I instantly felt calm and connected to spirit. Letting the fast-flowing water flow over my hand I felt and heard so many spirits, like conversation's passing through the water.

 *Spirit Message*

There would be no life with out water. So next time you see a puddle, glass of water, river have a moment because water is so much more than something to quench your thirst.

Think Like A Tree

Yes, I said think like a tree...
On one of my soul journeys, I was out immersed in nature and came across this beautiful tree. Here was this grand, strong beautiful and wise tree. Yet it needed supporting, a little love from us to keep him standing tall.

As I sat in awe of this magnificent tree, an old gentleman in spirit came and sat beside me. He said "I don't know why all you young folk don't think like a tree" his comments took me by surprise " Oh, ok and why is that?" I replied slightly confused.

He smiled and said "have you ever seen a perfect tree? Take that one for instance, look at him with is lumps and bumps, they all look different in their own way. Some have bumps and ridges, some have thick trunks and unruly roots, some have crocked and broken branches. But they all do the same thing, they give life, grow and look towards the light. They bloom where they are planed no matter the circumstances, they stand tall through every storm and they embrace their surroundings. They also welcome help and support".

He smiled at me "Trees don't care what other trees are doing. Just like I bet you have never heard a person say; my gosh that tree is ugly, too green or to tall. We just accept that is what a tree looks like. This is my advice my dear" and just like that he turned and walked away.

I have taken his advice and whenever I feel the weight of the world or I am about to embark on a new journey I think like a tree.

 *Spirit Message*

Think like a tree in every aspect of life. From starting a new venture, job, relationship or a new phase of your life. Accept who you are, love all your lumps and bumps, be willing to let people support and help you and bloom just like a tree, where you are planted. Let your wisdom guide you and don't let anyone bring you down, you can weather any storm just look towards the light and grow.

☾

Time To Smell The Roses

Today spirit are asking you to take time to smell the roses. This phrase has a deeper meaning when we relate roses to miracles, spirit and angelic encounters. The scent of roses in the air or around you, when there are no flowers near by, is a sign that spirit or an angel maybe trying to connect to you.

The smell of a rose is a very calming and comforting smell and is a blessing from the divine, and can be a sign that a blessing and prayer has been answered.

Roses also have powerful energy fields that vibrate at a high electrical frequency the highest of any flower on Earth. Because angelic energy also vibrates at a high rate, angels can connect easier with roses than with other flowers.

So next time you feel yourself surrounded by the sweet smell of roses, take a moment and ask spirit for a message and thank them for your blessings.

Window To Your Soul

What would you see if you looked through this window into your soul? I see endless possibilities, I see love yet to give and mountains yet to climb. We are never to old or to young to connect to our souls or start our soul journey. Sometimes we need to experience life before we can understand our soul path, connect to spirit and start our journey.

When I took this picture, I remember thinking how I wanted to find peace and be calm like the sea. Yet there was this thick wall in from of me just giving me a glimpse of the seas beauty. I have now found that peace and calmness and so much more as I deepen my journey with spirit and uncover layer by layer my beautiful soul. This is your opportunity to do the same.

Door To Spirit

Have you heard the saying, where one door closes another one opens? (this picture was taken on one of my many soul journeys, I couldn't see what was behind the door, it turned out to be a very steep winding staircase leading very closely to a mystical cove. It wasn't what I expected to see, but what I needed to experience).

I remember when I wanted to deepen my relationship with spirit and then suddenly I didn't feel as though I could connect. I felt as though the door had shut.

I hear the same from so many people, asking me why they feel they suddenly cannot connect to spirit. I remember asking spirit why and the response I received was:

"You are on a beautiful journey, stop rushing to get to the end point. Flowers don't rush to bloom, caterpillars only evolve into butterfly's when they are ready. Have patience and the result is something beautiful, something on a higher level. Wait and when the door opens again you will have a higher understanding of your connection to spirit and soul purpose."

It was at this point I became aware of a pattern emerging with spirit. When you want to deepen your connection and relationship, they will let it happen when you least expect it, but when you are ready.

When that door opens again, you will find that you are on a higher level with spirit and messages and signs come more easily to you. The door is never closed for very long, and usually closed because you need to rest, find and nurture yourself. When you are ready and the door opens again be prepared for the beauty that awaits you.

Spirit Message

Never give up on spirit. Patience is a beautiful virtue and the result well worth waiting for.

Past Present, Future

There is always a past, present and future. The past cannot be changed, it is yours to keep. Don't look BACK. Be present in the moment, take what you loved and learned from the past with you into the now. Don't let your past write your future because your future is bright.

I was walking in the woods on mother's day with my little ones. My youngest child has severe disabilities due to hospital negligence. He is nonverbal and struggles to walk properly, he really struggles and can find it quiet painful and overwhelming, resulting in him having a sensory meltdown and him screaming and throwing himself around on the floor. Due to his special needs he really struggles in new situations and surroundings.

On Mothers day he managed to walk up some steps (with a little love and guidance) and my gosh I was so unbelievably proud. He kept looking back after each step. I remember thinking how proud I was and how over joyed my family in spirit would be. Both he and I have come so far. In that moment I didn't let the sadness of my loved ones not being by my side to witness it, dampen such a beautiful and triumphant moment. Instead I stood in awe bursting with pride that they were with me in that moment and just as Blissful.

 *Spirit Message*

Your message is to go forth and explore the world, don't let past life experience or loss hold you back, your dreams are calling to you and together with spirit you can climb any mountain and surmount any obstacles.

Never Forgotten

One morning, I felt compelled to go for a walk and came across this beautiful tree. I felt the need to touch the ground, the energy was beautiful, and as I looked up there was a man from spirit leaning next to the tree. He was smiling and asked if it was obvious I could see him?

I explained that I can see hear and feel spirit. To which he replied "well let's hope my daughter can see me, she has been asking for a sign and she wants to see me. Did you know that blue bells are magical and linked to fairies?" No I didn't actually, I replied.

Spirit are constantly teaching me new things and what I have realised over the years, is that something small such as a single words that have no significant meaning to me, can mean something so significant and validating to the person I am reading for.

Moments later I could see a woman and a child walking towards the tree. As they approached the tree, I could now smell a man's aftershave. I heard the little girl shout daddy and run towards the tree where the man was now crouching down. The woman was slowly walking behind her. She looked at me, smiled and apologised for her little one running in front of me to the tree .I said it was fine and that she was only excited to see her dad.

The woman looked at me a little shocked. "How did you know. This is his tree?" I explained that I am a medium and was drawn to this tree and that for the past five minutes I had been chatting to him, while he had been waiting for her.

The woman smiled, and as tears fell down her face she said that she needed to hear that I could see her husband. We hugged and she dried her tears and explained that her daughter can see him and she so desperately wanted a sign from him. But didn't think it was possible. I told her where he was stood and to close her eyes and take a deep breath in. As she did her eyes opened and she said" I can smell him!" I smiled "Yes you can" I stood there in between them and gave her a message from him.

This was the tree where they laid his ashes. This tree was the dummy tree where they took her daughters dummies for the "fairies" to take away and where he always told her to come if she needed him. Someone once asked me if spirit can hear our thoughts, yes they can. They will give you a message when you least expect it but need it the most.

☽ *Spirit Message* ☾

Never lose hope , spirit will never forget about you, watch out for the signs, you will receive a sign from spirit when you least expect it but need it the most.

Lost

Have you ever felt lost? Like you didn't fit in, or know what you were supposed to be doing in life? Well the good news is that we all feel like this at some point in our lives! Welcome to the beautiful journey we call life. This picture was taken when I was out with the family and completely lost! I was in a maze and could not find my way out. I was the last one and I had completely lost my way. I kept coming to dead end after dead end. I was frustrated to say the least.

Normally I don't connect to spirit to help me win and finish the maze before my children. However this time I felt the need to connect and yes spirit was very amused. When I connected, this lovely gentle spirit popped up, he told me he was a gardener. He said that I was rushing to find the exit instead of enjoying the journey.

Exasperated I said "what journey? We are in a maze the whole point is who gets to the end the quickest? "Ah but you are wrong" he replied . Now I was confused. He stood there relaxed and simply replied "did you notice the lavender on the left and the wild garlic on your right? Did you notice the Robin that has been following you for the last 20 mins? If you had of noticed these, you would have noticed that they were leading you to the fountain, which essentially leads you to the exit".

"Oh right no" I replied slightly embarrassed. "I didn't" I replied sheepishly, "exactly my point" he smiled whilst leaning on his spiritual shovel. I thanked him and found my way to the fountain which, when I took a step back was a beautiful site and as he said led me to the exit.

This got me thinking, sometimes we are rushing to be someone we are not or so busy in life aiming to be the next Instagramer or reach a certain level of perfection. When we do this we can sometimes lose our way and selves along the way.

Your spirit message is to slow down and watch out for the simple things in life. Let life and spirit guide you. Do what makes you happy not what you think you should be doing or what other people think you should be doing.

Scars

Find your voice, our scars, make us who we are...

Hi beautiful soul, over the years I have realised that your soul isn't who you are in that moment. But is made up of layers. Every experience we face helps add another layer to your soul and shape who you are. This also includes experiences from your past lives.

Fear is a big part of soul growth, realising what your fears are, embracing the feeling, acknowledging it and then releasing it, letting go and breaking down those barriers and high walls fear built. Have your heard the saying our scars make us who we are?

This is so true. Some of us have physical scars, viable to the eye and others have invisible scars. These scars are experiences and should not define you but help you realise who you are. Help you find your voice and help you realise, that you have the strength and courage to move forward with your head held high. Your soul is growing. You are beautiful inside and out, so much stronger than you will ever know and very much loved.

No one is perfect, don't ever compare yourself to others. You are unique and so are your individual experiences. I grieve, love and learn differently to my family and friends and this normal.

I have a huge family in spirit and just because I can see, sense and feel them, doesn't detract from the good and bad days I have. I still love them, miss them and hold regrets because I am human. This is ok, its all part of our soul journey.

 *Spirit Message*

So next time you feel that you should be doing better, or grieve less or do something your not ready for, don't worry. You are doing amazing! Find your voice and when you are ready use it, don't be afraid. Let your soul shine and wear your scars with pride.

Find Your Inner child

Your inner child is the innocent aspect of yourself. The part that still believes in miracles, magic and approaches the world with wonder and awe.

Sometimes life can be so serious and we lose our sense of fun and wonder. Today spirit are asking you to find your inner child and start believing in the magic, that dreams really do come true and your miracle is waiting for you.

Don't lose faith, talk to spirit, angles and your spirit guides. Share with the universe your wildest dreams and let the magic unfold before your eyes. You have the power to change your life and it doesn't have to be all work and no play.

 *Spirit Message*

Let your imagination come to life and let the sound of laughter fill your ears and joy fill your heart.

Seeing Though The Dark

Sometimes we can feel a little lost in life. Imagine you are in a dark room and someone is asking you to find a book or a jumper.

You would struggle to find it. This can be the same at different phases through out our lives. Today spirit are asking you to take a moment, instead of rushing around the dark room trying to find something. Take a moment, sit and let your eyes adjust to the dark and your new environment and surroundings.

When you take this moment you will then be able to see a little clearer and see the light in the room or where the light switch is. This is the same process when connecting to your soul and your soul journey.

I hear so many people say they are struggling to connect to their soul path and that is because they are trying to look for something in the dark.

Find your light and turn it on the rest will come to you. Just like a moth to a flame. You will become a beacon of light and attract positive people, situations and moments in your life.

 *Spirit Message*

Take a few moments out of your busy day and just sit, close your eyes and let your mind wander to what makes you feel happy, what makes you feel loved, what makes you feel at peace and the answers you seek will follow.

☾

Your Soul Journey

Where is your soul journey leading you? Your soul has many beautiful layers, with each one comes new life lessons, challenges and growth. You can start your soul journey at any age and any stage of your life.

Your soul journey is a path of self discovery, it is not a race. I remember walking down these steps not knowing what to expect but excited and a little nervous as to where they would lead. Embrace every step, grow with every challenge and remember how far you have come, how truly amazing you are.

 Spirit Message ☾

Go forth explore, evolve, learn and grow, its your turn to take a step forward . You are strong, courageous and enough, there is nothing sent to you that you cannot overcome.

These steps led me to a place I hold dear to my heart and on to the next level of my soul journey. I remember that morning well, I couldn't decided if I wanted to go but spirit told me to go and explore to let my hair down and so I did. I met some beautiful spirits along the way.

☾

I Asked For A Sign

When I am on my travels, I always ask for a sign from spirit. I talk to spirit all of the time. The spirits I talk to, are not just my loved ones in spirit but your beautiful loved ones as well.

One morning, I was walking on a beautiful, peaceful and empty beach. The waves were crashing down and I asked spirit a question. As I did I felt I had a gentleman in spirit following me along the beach. I asked him gently to show himself. He obliged and said he was a father and he used to skim stones with his son on this very beach.

He told me to think of the answer in my head then look at my feet and I would find my sign. As I looked down I found this rock at my feet with a perfect heart naturally formed within the stone. I had my answer.

So I sat down in that very spot, talking to him. He explained that his spiritual love language was stones and that he had been showing his son signs in that way. But he sometimes felt that his son didn't connect to the signs he was trying to show him.

In that moment he truly touched my heart. We are not perfect, even in spirit. We are still learning, growing and evolving. communication is a two way street. I explained that we all have different love languages. Although he is trying to show his son signs with stones, a beautiful memory that they shared. His son might have other signs that he connects with.

I receive messages from people asking me why they are not receiving a sign from their loved ones in spirit. What they don't know, is that I receive messages from spirit asking me why their loved ones are not understanding or receiving signs from them.

It is important to understand that we all communicate in different and beautiful ways.

After my meeting with this lovely man, I left the beach. Four days later it was raining heavily, yet I felt the need to go for a walk along the same beach. I brought my daughter with me. As we walked along the beach embracing the freshness of the rain, we saw a man. He had a tripod and was taking pictures of the sunrise, he was the only one in the beach. I was about to leave when my daughter wanted to ask the man what he was doing. As we did I knew he was the spirits son. So I gave him a message from his dad and connected them there and then.

 *Spirit Message*

Open your mind to the signs and messages you receive, think deeply about your love language and that of your loved ones in spirit and you will see the signs you have been asking for.

Bliss Summers, international spiritual medium and manifestation coach. She has been connecting with spirit, spirit guides, and the angelic realm since she was a child and can see, hear, sense, and feel spirit. She has called on the divine light and has been providing messages from spirit for as long as she can remember. Bliss is also a successful author, having published many books, journals, and oracle cards. She also uses her gift to help others connect to spirit, find their soul path and manifest their dreams, through her audio programs, courses, and workshops.

For more information on Bliss's workshops, courses, books, journals, and oracle cards, please visit her website at www.positivelyspiritual.co.uk

Hi Beautiful Soul
Post pictures of your favourite images, pages,
affirmations and experiences related to this
book on social media using :

#BookOfLightOracle

So I can see them and share them on my page.

Thank you lovely xx

www.positivelyspiritual.co.uk

Made in the USA
Middletown, DE
09 August 2022